The Ernest Newton Community Song Book

Alphabetical Index

	Page
Abide with Me	104
A-Hunting we will go	62
All Through the Night	42
Aloha Oe	87
Alouette	88
Animals went in two by two, The	71
Annie Laurie	27
A-Roving	46
Auld Lang Syne	28
Bailiff's Daughter of Islington, The	2
Barbara Allen	3
Bay of Biscay, The	47
Blow the man Down	48
Blue Bells of Scotland, The	30
British Grenadiers, The	49
Camptown Races	72
Canadian Boat Song, A	89
Clementine	90
Cockles and Mussels	35
Cock Robin	91
Come back to Erin	36
Come, Landlord fill the Flowing Bowl	61
Come, Lasses and Lads	4
Dame! get up and bake your pies	101
Down among the dead men	64
Drink to me only with thine eyes	5
Early one morning	6
Farmer's Boy, The	7
Fine Old English Gentleman, The	8
For he's a jolly good fellow	65
Gather ye Rosebuds while ye may	9
Glorious things of Thee are spoken	105
Glory to Thee, my God	110
God bless the Prince of Wales	43
God save the Queen	10
Golden Slumbers	11
Good-night, Ladies	92
Grace	106
Green Grow the Rashes, O!	29
Hark the bonny Christ Church Bells	100
Harp That Once, The	38
Haste thee, Nymph	100
Haul on the Bowlin'	50
Heart of oak	51
Here's a health unto His Majesty	12
Here's to the Maiden of bashful fifteen	66
Hickory, Dickory, Dock!	101
It was a Lover and his Lass	13
Jack and Jill	102
John Brown's body	78

	Page
John Peel	67
Keel Row, The	93
Killarney	39
Lass of Richmond Hill, The	14
Last Rose of Summer, The	40
Lincolnshire Poacher, The	16
Little Bo-Peep	102
Little Brown Jug, The	70
Loch Lomond	32
Lo! Heaven and Earth	107
Maple Leaf for Ever	94
Marching through Georgia	74
Men of Harlech	44
Mermaid, The	52
Miller of the Dee, The	17
Minstrel Boy, The	41
My Bonnie is over the ocean	79
My old Kentucky home	76
Nearer my God to Thee	108
O come, all ye Faithful	109
O God our help in ages past	110
Oh! Dear! What can the matter be?	18
Oh! the Oak and the Ash	19
Old folks at home, The	82
Old Hundredth	108
Pack up your troubles in your old kitbag	54
Polly-Wolly-Doodle	80
Poor Old Joe	83
Praise, my soul,, the King of Heaven	111
Rio Grande	56
Rock-a-bye, Baby	103
Rule Britannia	20
Sally in our Alley	21
Scots, wha hae wi' Wallace bled	33
Shenandoah	57
Since first I saw your Face	22
So early in de morning	86
Some folks do	98
Soldiers' Chorus, The (Faust)	58
Sweet and Low	23
Sweet Genevieve	96
Swing Low, Sweet Chariot	84
There is a Tavern in the Town	68
Uncle Tom Cobleigh	26
Vesper Hymn	112
Vicar of Bray, The	24
What shall we do with the drunken sailor?	60
When good King Arthur ruled this Land	103
Where are you going, my Pretty Maid?	99
Ye Banks and Braes	34

Keith Prowse Music Publishing Co. Ltd
distributed by
EMI Music Publishing Co. Ltd., 138-140 Charing Cross Road, London WC2H 0LD

The Bailiff's Daughter of Islington

Traditional

3.
"Before I give you a penny, sweetheart,
　Pray tell me where you were born;"
"At Islington, kind sir," she said,
　"Where I have had many a scorn"
"I prythee, sweetheart, tell to me,
　O' tell me if you know
The bailiff's daughter of Islington?"
　"She is dead, sir, long ago."

4.
"If she be dead, then take my horse,
　My saddle and bridle also,
For I will to some far country,
　Where no man shall me know."
"Oh stay, oh stay, thou goodly youth,
　She standeth by thy side!
She is here, alive, she is not dead,
　And ready to be thy bride!"

This arrangement Copyright 1927 by Keith Prowse & Co., Ltd.

Barbara Allen

3
So slowly, slowly she came up,
And slowly she came nigh him,
And all she said when there she came,
"Young man, I think you're dying!"

4
When he was dead and laid in grave,
Her heart was struck with sorrow;
"O mother dear! Come make my bed,
For I shall die tomorrow."

Come, Lasses and Lads

Traditional

5. Now there they did stay the whole of the day,
   And tired the fiddler quite,
   With dancing and play, without any pay,
   From morning unto night.
   They told the fiddler then
   They'd pay him for his play;
   And each a twopence, twopence, twopence,
   Gave him, and went away.

6. "Good-night," says Harry, "Good-night," says Mary,
   "Good-night," says Dolly to John;
   "Good-night," says Sue, "Good-night," says Hugh,
   "Good-night," says every one.
   Some walked, and some did run,
   Some loitered on the way;
   And bound themselves by kisses twelve
   To meet the next holiday.

This arrangement Copyright 1927 by Keith Prowse & Co., Ltd.

Drink to me only with thine eyes

This arrangement Copyright 1927 by Keith Prowse & Co. Ltd.

Early one morning

1. Early one morning, just as the sun was rising, I heard a maid sing in the valley below; "Oh! don't deceive me, Oh! never leave me, How could you use a poor maiden so?"
2. Oh! gay is the garland, and fresh are the roses I've cull'd from the garden to bind on thy brow;

3. Remember the vows that you made to your Mary,
Remember the bow'r where you vow'd to be true;
   "Oh! don't deceive me *etc*"

4. Thus sang the poor maiden, her sorrow bewailing,
Thus sang the poor maid in the valley below —
   "Oh! don't deceive me *etc*"

The Farmer's Boy

Old English Song

4.
The farmer's wife cried, "Try the lad,
   Let him no longer seek;"
"Yes, father, do!" the daughter cried,
   While the tears rolled down her cheek.
"For those who would work it's hard to want,
   And wander for employ.
Don't let him go, but let him stay
   And be a farmer's boy.

5.
The farmer's boy grew up a man,
   And the good old couple died;
They left the lad the farm they had,
   And the daughter for his bride.
Now the lad that was, and the farm now has,
   Often thinks and smiles with joy,
And blesses the day he came that way
   To be a farmer's boy.

This arrangement Copyright 1927 by Keith Prowse & Co., Ltd.

The Fine Old English Gentleman

Moderato

1. I'll sing you a good old song, That was made by a good old pate, Of a fine old English Gentleman Who had an old estate; And who kept up his old mansion At a bountiful old rate, With a good old porter to relieve The old poor at his gate, Like a fine old English Gentleman, One of the olden time.

2. His Hall, so old, was hung about With pikes and guns and bows, And sword and good old bucklers Which had stood against old foes; 'Twas there "His Worship" sat in state In doublet and trunk hose, And quaff'd his cup of good old sack, To warm his good old nose, Like a fine old English Gentleman, One of the olden time.

3. His custom was, when Christmas came,
   To bid his friends repair
   To his old hall, where feast and ball
   For them he did prepare;
   And tho' the rich he entertained,
   He ne'er forgot the poor;
   Nor were there any destitute
   E'er driven from the door
   Of this good old English Gentleman,
   One of the olden time.

4. But time, though sweet, is strong in flight,
   And years roll swiftly by;
   And Autumn's falling leaves proclaim'd
   This good old man must die.
   He laid him down right tranquilly
   Gave up life's latest sigh,
   A mournful silence reign'd around,
   And tears bedewed each eye
   For this fine old English Gentleman,
   One of the olden time.

Gather ye rose-buds while you may

ROBERT HERRICK
(1591-1674)

WILLIAM LAWES
(1590-1645)

1. Gather ye rose-buds while ye may, Old time is still a-flying; And this same flower that smiles to-day, To-morrow will be dying.
2. glorious lamp of heaven, the Sun, The higher he's a-getting, The sooner will his race be run, And nearer he's to setting.

3
That age is best, which is the first,
When youth and blood are warmer;
But being spent, the worse and worst
Times still succeed the former.

4
Then be not coy, but use your time,
And while ye may, go marry;
For having lost but once your prime,
You may for ever tarry.

This arrangement Copyright 1927 by Keith Prowse & Co., Ltd.

God save the Queen

1. God save our gracious Queen, Long live our noble Queen, God save the Queen. Send her, victorious, Happy and glorious, Long to reign over us, God save the Queen.

2. O Lord our God arise, Scatter her enemies, And make them fall! Confound their politics, Frustrate their knavish tricks, On Thee our hopes we fix, God save us all.

3
Thy choicest gifts in store,
On her be pleased to pour,
Long may she reign.
May she defend our laws,
And ever give us cause
To sing with heart and voice,
God save the Queen!

This arrangement Copyright 1927 by Keith Prowse & Co. Ltd.

Golden Slumbers

A 17th Century Lullaby

This arrangement Copyright 1927 by Keith Prowse & Co., Ltd.

Here's a Health unto His Majesty

By JEREMY SAVILE

This arrangement Copyright 1927 by Keith Prowse & Co., Ltd.

It was a lover and his lass

The Lass of Richmond Hill

J. HOOK

1. On Rich-mond Hill there lives a lass, More bright than May-day morn, Whose charms all oth-er maids sur-pass, A rose with-out a thorn. This

zeph-yrs gay that fan the air, And wan-ton through the grove, O whis-per to my charm-ing fair, I die for her I love. This

The Lincolnshire Poacher

Old English

4.
I threw him on my shoulder, and then we trudgéd home,
We took him to a neighbour's house and sold him for a crown,
We sold him for a crown, my boys, but I need not tell you where.
  Oh, tis my delight etc.

5.
Success to every gentleman that lives in Lincolnshire,
Success to every poacher that wants to sell a hare,
Bad luck to every gamekeeper that will not sell his deer.
  Oh, tis my delight etc.

This arrangement Copyright 1927 by Keith Prowse & Co., Ltd

The Miller of the Dee

A 17th Century Song

This arrangement Copyright 1927 by Keith Prowse & Co., Ltd.

Oh! the Oak and the Ash

17th Century

Sally in our Alley

HENRY CAREY

Since first I saw your face

THOMAS FORD (1580-1648)

The Vicar of Bray

3. When William was our king declared,
   To ease a nation's grievance,
   With this new wind about I steer'd
   And swore to him allegiance;
   Old principles I did revoke,
   Set conscience at a distance;
   Passive obediance was a joke,
   A jest was non-resistance.
   And this is law, etc.

4. When gracious Anne became our Queen,
   The Church of England's glory,
   Another face of things was seen,
   And I became a Tory;
   Occasional Conformists base,
   I damn'd their moderation,
   And thought the church in danger was,
   By such prevarication.
   And this is law, etc.

5. When George in pudding-time came o'er,
   And moderate men look'd big, sir,
   I turned a cat-in-a-pan once more,
   And so became a Whig, sir;
   And thus, preferment I procured,
   From our new faith's defender,
   And almost every day abjured
   The Pope and the Pretender.
   And this is law, etc

6. The Illustrious house of Hanover
   And Protestant succession,
   To these I do allegiance swear,
   While they can keep possession;
   For in my faith and loyalty
   I never more will falter,
   And George my lawful King shall be,
   Until the times do alter.
   And this is law, etc

Uncle Tom Cobleigh
(WIDDICOMBE FAIR)

Old Devonshire Song

3. Then Friday came, and Saturday noon,
   All along, down along, out along lee;
   But Tom Pearse's old mare have not trotted home,
   With Bill Brewer &c. *Chorus.*

4. So Tom Pearse he got up to the top o' the hill,
   All along, down along, out along lee;
   And he seed his old mare down a making her will,
   With Bill Brewer &c. *Chorus.*

5. So Tom Pearse's old mare her took sick and died,
   All along, down along, out along lee;
   And Tom he sat down on a stone, and he cried
   With Bill Brewer &c. *Chorus.*

6. But this isn't the end o' this shocking affair,
   All along, down along, out along lee;
   Nor, though they be dead, of the horrid career
   Of Bill Brewer &c. *Chorus.*

7. When the wind whistles cold on the moor of a night,
   All along, down along, out along lee;
   Tom Pearse's old mare doth appear, gashly white,
   With Bill Brewer &c. *Chorus.*

8. And all the long night be heard skirling and groans,
   All along, down along, out along lee;
   From Tom Pearse's old mare in her rattling bones,
   And Bill Brewer &c. *Chorus.*

This arrangement Copyright 1927 by Keith Prowse & Co., Ltd.
Tune and words by permission of Messrs Methuen & Co., Ltd.

Annie Laurie

This arrangement Copyright 1927 by Keith Prowse & Co., Ltd.

Auld Lang Syne

Green grow the rashes, O!

3. And you sae douce, wha sneer at this,
   Ye're nought but senseless asses, O!
   The wisest man the warld e'er saw,
   He dearly lo'ed the lasses, O!
       Green grow the rashes, O! etc.

4. Auld Nature swears, the lovely dears
   Her noblest works she classes, O!
   Her 'prentice han' she tried on man,
   An' then she made the lasses, O!
       Green grow the rashes, O! etc.

The Blue Bell of Scotland.

Words by Mrs GRANT

Oh! what, tell me what if your Highland lad be slain?
Oh! what, tell me what if your Highland lad be slain?
Oh, no! true love will be his guard and bring him safe again,
For it's oh! my heart would break if my Highland lad were slain.
Oh, no! true love will be his guard, *etc.*

Loch Lomond

This arrangement Copyright 1927 by Keith Prowse & Co., Ltd.

Scots, wha hae wi' Wallace bled

Cockles and Mussels

Come back to Erin

By CLARIBEL

1. Come back to E-rin, Ma-vour-neen, Ma-vour-neen! Come back A-roon to the land of thy birth; Come with the sham-rock and spring-time, Ma-vour-neen, And its Kil-lar-ney shall ring with our mirth.
2. O-ver the green sea, Ma-vour-neen, Ma-vour-neen, Long shone the white sail that bore thee a-way. Ri-ding the white waves that fair summer morn-in', Just like a May-flower a-float on the bay.
3. O may the An-gels, a-wak-in' and sleep-in', Watch o'er my bird in the land far a-way; And it's my prayers will con-sign to their keep-in', Care o' my jew-el by night and by day.

Sure, when we lent ye to beau-ti-ful Eng-land, Lit-tle we thought of the lone win-ter days; Lit-tle we thought of the hush of the star shine, O-ver the moun-tain, the Bluffs and the Braes!

Oh! but my heart sank when clouds came between us, Like a grey cur-tain the rain fall-ing down, Hid from my red eyes the path o'er the o-cean, Far, far a-way where my Col-leen had flown.

When by the fire-side I watch the bright em-bers, Then all my heart flies to Eng-land and thee, Crav-in' to know if my dar-ling re-mem-bers, Or if her thoughts may be cross-in' to me.

Then Come back to E-rin, Ma-vour-neen, Ma-vour-neen, Come back a-gain to the land of thy birth Come back to E-rin, Ma-vour-neen, Mavour-neen, And its Kil-lar-ney shall ring with our mirth.

D. 𝄋

The Harp that once

THOMAS MOORE
Irish Melody

Andante moderato. Key D.

1. The harp that once thro' Ta - ra's halls, The Soul of Mu-sic shed, Now hangs as mute on Ta - ra's walls As if that soul were fled. So sleeps the pride of form-er days, So glo-ry's thrill is o'er; And hearts that once beat high for praise Now feel that pulse no more.

2. No more to chiefs and la - dies bright The harp of Ta - ra swells; The chord a - lone that breaks the night Its tale of ru - in tells. Thus Free-dom now so sel-dom wakes, The on - ly throb she gives Is when some heart in - dig - nant breaks To show that still she lives.

This arrangement Copyright 1927 by Keith Prowse & Co., Ltd.

Killarney

Words by E. FALCONER
Music by BALFE

Moderato — Key E♭

1. By Killarney's lakes and fells, Em'rald isles and winding bays. Mountain paths and woodland dells, Mem'ry ever fondly strays. Bounteous nature loves all lands, Beauty wanders ev'rywhere. Footprints leaves on many strands, But her home is surely there! Angels fold their wings and rest, In that Eden of the West; Beauty's home, Killarney, Heav'ns reflex, Killarney.

2. No place else can charm the eye, With such bright and varied tints. Ev'ry rock that you pass by, Verdure broiders or besprints. Virgin there the green grass grows, Ev'ry morn Spring's natal day; Bright hued berries daff the snows, Smiling Winter's frown away. Angels, often pausing there, Doubt if Eden were more fair; Beauty's home, Killarney, Heav'ns reflex, Killarney.

The Last Rose of Summer

Words by THOMAS MOORE

1. 'Tis the last rose of sum-mer Left bloom-ing a-lone, All her love-ly com-pan-ions Are fa-ded and gone; No flow'r of her kin-dred, No rose-bud is nigh,— To re-flect back her blush-es, Or give sigh for sigh.

2. I'll not leave thee, thou lone one, To pine on the stem, Since the love-ly are sleep-ing, Go sleep thou with them. Thus kind-ly I scat-ter Thy leaves o'er the bed, Where thy mates of the gar-den Lie scent-less and dead.

The Minstrel Boy

MOORE (Irish Melodies)

All through the night

Words by T. OLIPHANT.
Andante
Welsh Tune

Key G

1. While the moon her watch is keep-ing, All through the night;
2. Fond-ly, then, I dream of thee, love, All through the night;

While the wea-ry world is sleep-ing, All through the night;
Wak-ing, still thy form I see, love, All through the night;

O'er my bo-som gent-ly steal-ing, Vis-ions of de-light re-veal-ing,
When this mor-tal coil is o-ver, Will thy gen-tle spi-rit hov-er

Breathes a pure and ho-ly feel-ing, All through the night.
O'er the bed where sleeps thy lov-er All through the night.

God Bless the Prince of Wales

Words by GEORGE LINLEY

Music by BRINLEY RICHARDS

Men of Harlech

Words by EDWARD LOCKTON

Welsh Melody

1. Men of Har-lech are ye wa-king? Sax-on hosts your hills are sha-king, Proud-ly now your swords be ta-king Gath-er in your might! Hark a thou-sand voi-ces call ye, Let old he-ro hearts en-thrall ye, Shall the thought of Death ap-pal ye? Hast-en to the fight!

2. Ne'er an a-lien hand shall hold ye, Ne'er shall chains of serf-dom fold ye, Have the moun-tains nev-er told ye? 'Har-lech men are free!' Foes may come, but ye shall stay them, Fierce and ruth-less ye shall slay them, In the dust your swords shall lay them, Vic-tors ye shall be!

This arrangement Copyright 1927 by Keith Prowse & Co., Ltd.

45

With your trum-pets sound-ing, Wild - ly forth be bound-ing,
Spear on spear is crash-ing, Man on man is dash-ing,

On - ward go to meet the foe, The ty - rant band sur-round-ing; Your
Loud and strong lift up your song While sword on sword is clash-ing; "No

an - cient ban - ners wav-ing o'er ye, Rank on rank fall back be - fore ye,
fet - ter shall be ours, no hal - ter, Ne'er a foe our laws shall al - ter,

March to vic - t'ry, march to glo - ry, Harlech, show your might!
Let them come, we shall not fal - ter, Harlech men are free!"

A-Roving

Moderato   *Sea Shanty*

Key E♭.

In Amsterdam there lived a maid, And she was tall and fair; Her eyes were blue, her cheeks were red, And she had auburn hair. But I'll go no more a-roving with you, fair maid. A-roving, a-roving, Since roving's been my ruin. I'll go no more a-roving with you, fair maid.

The Bay of Biscay

ANDREW CHERRY
J. DAVY

Moderato

1. Loud roar'd the dreadful thunder, The rain, a deluge show'rs, The clouds were rent asunder By lightning's vivid powers. The night was drear and dark, Our poor devoted bark Till next day there she lay In the Bay of Biscay, O!

2. Now dash'd upon the billow, Her op'ning timbers creak, Each fears a wat'ry pillow, None stop the dreadful leak. To cling to slipp'ry shrouds, Each breathless seaman crowds, As she lay till next day In the Bay of Biscay, O!

3. At length the wish'd for morrow
Broke thro' the hazy sky,
Absorb'd in silent sorrow,
Each heav'd a bitter sigh.
The dismal wreck to view
Struck horror in the crew,
As she lay all that day
In the Bay of Biscay, O!

4. Her yielding timbers sever,
Her pitchy seams are rent,
When heaven all bounteous ever,
Its boundless mercy sent.
A sail in sight appears,
We hail her with three cheers;
Now we sail, with the gale,
From the Bay of Biscay, O!

Blow the man down!

Moderato — Sea Shanty

Key E♭

1. Oh, blow the man down bul-lies, Blow the man down, Oh, way-ay! blow the man down! Oh, blow the man down bul-lies, blow him a-way, Oh, gim-me some time to blow the man down.

2. The mack'rel was sing-ing, "I'm king of the sea," Oh, way-ay! blow the man down! Oh, give me a pull, We're bound for to go, Oh, gim-me some time to blow the man down.

3.
Oh! blow the man down, bullies, blow the man down!
Oh! way-ay! blow the man down!
Oh! give her a pull and we'll send her along,
Oh! gimme sometime to blow the man down.

4.
As I was a-walking down Rotherhithe street,
Oh! way-ay! blow the man down!
A pretty young creature, I chanced for to meet,
Oh! gimme sometime to blow the man down.

The British Grenadiers

Tempo di Marcia

Key G

1. Some talk of Al - ex - an - der, And some of Her - cu - les, Of Hec - tor and Ly - san - der, And such great names as these; But of all the world's brave he - roes, There's none that can com - pare, With a tow, row, row, row, row, row, To the Brit - ish Gren - a - diers. 1. None

2. of those an - cient he - roes E'er saw a can - non - ball, Or knew the force of pow - der, To slay their foes with - al; But our brave boys do know it, And ban - ish all their fears, Sing - ing

   of those an - cient ... let us fill a bump - er, And drink a health to those Who car - ry caps and pou - ches, And wear the loop - ed clothes; May they and their com - man - ders Live hap - py all their years, With a

2. Then

This arrangement Copyright 1927 by Keith Prowse & Co., Ltd.

Haul on the Bowlin'

Moderato — Key F

1. Haul on the bowlin', the Bully ship's a rollin',
2. Haul on the bowlin', the fore and maintop bowlin',

Haul on the bowlin', haul away, Jo!
Haul on the bowlin', haul away, Jo!

CHORUS

Heave, heave 'er up, We'll either break or strand her, A-way, haul away! Haul away, Jo!

3
Haul on the bowlin', the packet is a rollin',
Haul on the bowlin', Haul away, Jo!
Heave, heave 'er up, etc.

4
Haul on the bowlin', the skipper he's a-growlin',
Haul on the bowlin', Haul away, Jo!
Heave, heave 'er up, etc.

5
Haul on the bowlin', to London we are goin',
Haul on the bowlin', Haul away, Jo!
Heave, heave 'er up, etc.

6
Haul on the bowlin', the main-topgallant howlin',
Haul on the bowlin', Haul away, Jo!
Heave, heave 'er up, etc.

This arrangement Copyright 1927 by Keith Prowse & Co., Ltd.

Heart of Oak

DAVID GARRICK 1750
WILLIAM BOYCE
Moderato
Key B♭

1. Come, cheer up my lads, 'tis to glory we steer, To add something new to this wonderful year; To honour we call you, not press you like slaves, For who are so free as the sons of the waves.
Heart of Oak are our ships, Jolly tars are our men, We always are ready, Steady, boys, steady! We'll fight and we'll conquer again and again.

2. We ne'er see our foes, but we wish them to stay, They never see us but they wish us away, If they run, why we follow, and run them ashore, For if they won't fight us, we cannot do more.

3. Still Britain shall triumph, her ships plough the sea,
Her standard be Justice, her watchword 'Be free;'
Then cheer up, my lads, with one heart let us sing,
Our soldiers, our sailors, our statesmen, our King.
Heart of Oak etc.

This arrangement Copyright 1927 by Keith Prowse & Co., Ltd.

The Mermaid

Traditional

Moderato Key D

1. One Friday morn when we set sail, And our ship not far from land, We there did espy a fair pretty maid, With a comb and a glass in her hand, her hand, her hand, With a comb and a glass in her hand. While the

up starts the captain of our gallant ship, And a brave young man was he; I've a wife and a child in fair Bristol town, But a widow I fear she will be, will be, will be, But a widow I fear she will be. For the

This arrangement Copyright 1927 by Keith Prowse & Co., Ltd.

rag-ing seas did roar, ——— And the storm-y winds did blow, While we jol-ly sail-or boys were sitt-ing up a-loft, And the land lub-bers ly-ing down be-low, be-low, be-low, And the land lub-bers ly-ing down be-low. ——— 2. Then

2
Then up starts the mate of our gallant ship,
And a bold young man was he;
Oh! I have a wife in fair Portsmouth town,
But a widow I fear she will be, &c.
For the raging seas, &c.

4
Then up starts the cook of our gallant ship,
And a gruff old soul was he;
Oh! I have a wife in fair Plymouth town,
But a widow I fear she will be, &c.
For the raging seas, &c.

5
And then up spoke the little cabin-boy,
And a pretty little boy was he:
Oh! I am more griev'd for my daddy and my mammy,
Than you for your wives all three, &c.
For the raging seas, &c.

6
Then three times round went our gallant ship,
And three times round went she;
For the want of a life-boat they all went down,
And she sank to the bottom of the sea, &c.
For the raging seas, &c.

Pack up your troubles in your old kit-bag

Words by GEORGE ASAF
Music by FELIX POWELL

Tempo di marcia

1. Pri - vate Perks is a fun - ny lit - tle cod - ger With a
2. Pri - vate Perks went a marching in - to Flanders With his
3. Pri - vate Perks he came back from Bosche shooting With his

smile — a fun - ny smile Five feet none, he's an art - ful lit - tle
smile — his fun - ny smile He was lov'd by the privates and com-
smile — his fun - ny smile.... Round his home he then set a - bout re-

dod - ger With a smile — a sun - ny smile Flush or broke, hell
-man - ders For his smile — his sun - ny smile When a throng of
-cruit - ing With his smile — his sun - ny smile He told all his

have his lit - tle joke, He can't be sup - press'd All the
Ger - mans came a - long, With a might - y swing, Perks yell'd
pals, the short, the tall, What a time he'd had; And as

Copyright MCMXV in the United States of America by Francis, Day & Hunter
Reproduced by kind permission of the publishers. Messrs Francis, Day & Hunter Ltd.

55

oth-er fel-lows have to grin When he gets this off his chest, sing } (Shout) Hi!
out "This lit-tle bunch is mine! Keep your heads down, boys, and
each en-list-ed like a man, Priv-ate Perks said, "Now, my lad,

CHORUS *mp 2nd time*
Well marked
"Pack up your troubles in your old kit-bag, And smile, smile, smile

While you've a lu-ci-fer to light your fag, Smile, boys, that's the style

What's the use of wor-ry-ing? It nev-er was worth while, so Pack up your

troubles in your old kit-bag and smile, smile, smile" smile"
Fine

Rio Grande

Moderato

Key E♭

SOLO
|m :r :d |s :-:m |r :d :r |d :-:- |

CHORUS
|s :-:-|-:m :l |

1. Where are you goin' to, my pretty maid? Way,—— Heigh-
2. Jol-ly our ship and jol-ly our crew, Way,—— Heigh-

SOLO
|s :-:-|-:d' :-t |l :l :l |s :-:m |f :s :f |m :-:d |m :r :d |r :s :- |

-Ho!—— Oh,—— where are you goin' to my pret-ty maid? We're bound for the Ri-o
-Ho!—— Oh,—— jol-ly our mate, our good skipper too,

CHORUS
|d :-:-|-:d :r |m :-:-|-:d :r |d :-:-|-:-:s |s :-:-|-:m :l |s :-:-|-:d' :-t |

Grande. Then a-way,—— Heigh-Ho! A-way,—— Heigh-Ho! Sing

|l :-:l |s :-:m |f :-:s :f |m :-:d .r |m :r :d |r :s :- |d :-:-|-:- :|

fare you well, My bon-nie young girl, For we're bound for the Ri-o Grande.——

D.S.

Shenandoah

Sea Shanty

Slow

1. Shen-an-doah, I love your daugh-ter, A-way, you roll-ing riv-er! Shen-an-doah, I long to hear you; A-way we're bound a way 'Cross the wide Mis-sou-ri.

2. The ship sails free, a gale is blow-ing, A-way, you roll-ing riv-er! The bra-ces taut, the sheets a-flow-ing, A-

3
Shenandoah, I'll ne'er forget you,
Away, you rolling river!
Till I die, I'll love you ever,
Away, we're bound away
'Cross the wide Missouri.

The Soldiers' Chorus (Faust)

CHARLES GOUNOD

Tempo marziale

Glo-ry and love to the men of old! Their sons may copy their virtues bold, Cour-age in heart and a sword in hand, Ready to fight, or ready to die for Fa - ther-land! Who needs bidding to dare, by a trumpet blown? Who lacks pi-ty to spare when the field is won?

59

Who would fly from a foe___ if a-lone or last?___ And boast he was true, as coward might do, when peril is past? Glo-ry and love to the men of old!___ Their sons may copy their virtues bold, Cour-age in heart and a sword in hand, Ready to fight for Fa-ther-land, or ready to die for Fa-ther-land, or ready to die,___ or ready to die,___ for Fa-ther-land.___

What shall we do with a drunken sailor?

Allegretto   Sea Shanty

1. What shall we do with a drunk-en sail-or? What shall we do with a drunk-en sail-or? What shall we do with a drunk-en sail-or? Ear-ly in the morn-ing.
2. Soak him with a hose-pipe un-til he is so-ber, Soak him with a hose-pipe un-til he is so-ber, Soak him with a hose-pipe un-til he is so-ber, Ear-ly in the morn-ing.

Hoo-ray and up she ris-es, Hoo-ray and up she ris-es, Hoo-ray and up she ris-es, Ear-ly in the morn-ing.

D.S.

Come, Landlord, Fill The Flowing Bowl

Old English

In march time

1. Come, land-lord, fill the flow-ing bowl, Un-til it doth run o-ver, For tonight we'll mer-ry be, For tonight we'll mer-ry be, For tonight we'll mer-ry be, To morrow we'll be so-ber, so-ber, so-ber, For tonight we'll mer-ry be, For tonight we'll mer-ry be, For tonight we'll mer-ry be, To-mor-row we'll be so-ber.

2. The man that drink-eth small beer, And goes to bed quite so-ber, Fades as the leaves do fade, Fades as the leaves do fade, Fades as the leaves do fade, That drop off in Oc-to-ber- to-ber- to-ber, Fades as the leaves do fade, Fades as the leaves do fade, Fades as the leaves do fade, That drop off in Oc-to-ber.

3. The man who drink-eth strong beer, And goes to bed right mel-low, Lives as he ought to live, Lives as he ought to live, Lives as he ought to live, And dies a jolly good fel-low, fel-low, fel-low, Lives as he ought to live, Lives as he ought to live, Lives as he ought to live, And dies a jolly good fel-low.

4. But he who drinks just what he likes,
   And getteth half seas over,
   Will live until he die perhaps,
   And then lie down in clover.

5. But he who kisses a pretty girl,
   And goes and tells his mother,
   Ought to have his lips cut off,
   And never kiss another.

This arrangement Copyright 1927 by Keith Prowse & Co., Ltd.

A - Hunting we will go

Words by HENRY FIELDING

Traditional

Allegro

1. The dusky night rides down the sky, And ushers in _____ the morn; _____ The hounds all join in glorious cry, The hounds all join in glorious cry, The

   wife around her husband throws Her arms, and begs _____ him stay; _____ "My dear, it rains, it hails, it snows, My dear, it rains, it hails, it snows, You

   brushing fox in yonder wood, Secure to find _____ we seek; _____ For why, I carried, For why, I carried, sound and good, A

This arrangement Copyright 1927 by Keith Prowse & Co., Ltd.

63

hunts-man winds his horn, The hunts-man winds his
will not hunt to-day, You will not hunt to-
cart-load there last week, A cart-load there last

horn. Then a hunt-ing we will
day" But a hunt-ing we will go, A
week. And a hunt-ing we will

hunt-ing we will go, A hunt-ing we will

go, A hunt-ing we will go.
2. The
3. A

Fine

4. Away he goes, he flies the rout,
   Their steeds they soundly switch;
   Some are thrown in, and some thrown out,
   And some thrown in the ditch.
   But a-hunting we will go.

5. At length his strength to faintness worn,
   Poor Reynard ceases flight;
   Then hungry, homeward we return,
   To feast away the night.
   Then a-drinking we do go.

Down among the dead men

"DYER"
Allegro vigoroso — Key E♭ — About 1700

1. Here's a health to the King, and a lasting peace,
To faction an end, to wealth increase,
Come let's drink it while we have breath,
For there's no drinking after death,
And he that will this health deny,
Down among the dead men,
Down among the dead men,
Down, down, down, down,
Down among the dead men let him lie!

2. Let charming beauty's health go round,
In whom celestial joys are found,
May confusion still pursue
The selfish woman-hating crew;
And they that woman's health deny,
Down among the dead men,
Down among the dead men,
Down, down, down, down,
Down among the dead men let them lie!

3. In smiling Bacchus' joys I'll roll,
Deny no pleasure to my soul,
Let Bacchus' health now briskly move,
For Bacchus is a friend of Love.
And he that will this health deny,
Down among the dead men let him lie!

4. May love and wine their rights maintain,
And their united pleasures reign,
While Bacchus' treasure crown the board,
We'll sing the joys that both afford;
And they that won't with us comply,
Down among the dead men let them lie!

This arrangement Copyright 1927 by Keith Prowse & Co., Ltd.

For he's a jolly good fellow

Here's to the maiden of bashful fifteen

Words by SHERIDAN
Music by THOMAS LINLEY

Moderato. Key D.

1. Here's to the maiden of bashful fifteen, Here's to the widow of fifty; Here's to the flaunting extravagant queen, And here's to the house-wife that's thrifty. Let the toast pass, Drink to the lass, I warrant she'll prove an excuse for the glass, Let the toast pass, Drink to the lass, I warrant she'll prove an excuse for the glass.

2. Here's to the charmer whose dimples we prize, Here's to the damsel with none, Sir; Here's to the girl with a pair of blue eyes, And here's to the nymph with but one, Sir.

3. Here's to the maid with a bosom of snow, Now to her brown as a berry; Here's to the wife with a face full of woe, And here's to the girl that is merry.

John Peel

Moderato. Key E♭

1. Do ye ken John Peel with his coat so grey, Do ye ken John Peel at the break of the day, Do ye ken John Peel when he's far, far away, With his hounds and his horn in the morning?

For the sound of his horn brought me from my bed, And the cry of his hounds which he oft-times led; Peel's stal-ly-ho would a-waken the dead, Or the fox from his lair in the morn-ing.

2. Yes I ken John Peel and Ru-by too, Ranter and Ring-wood, Bell-man and True, From a find to a check, from a check to a view, From a view to a death in the morning.

3. Then here's to John Peel from my heart and soul, Let's drink to his health, let's fin-ish the bowl, We'll fol-low John Peel through fair and thro' foul, If we want a good hunt in the morning.

4. Do ye ken John Peel with his coat so gray?
He lived at Troutbeck once on a day;
Now he has gone far, far, far away,
We shall ne'er hear his voice in the morning.
For the sound of his horn. *etc.*

This arrangement Copyright 1927 by Keith Prowse & Co., Ltd.

There is a tavern in the town

Adapted from A Cornish Folk-Song.

Moderato. Key C.

1. There is a tav-ern in the town, in the town, And there my dear love sits him down, sits him down, And drinks his wine 'mid laugh-ter free, And nev-er, nev-er thinks of me.

left me for a dam-sel dark, dam-sel dark, Each Fri-day night they used to spark, used to spark, And now my love once true to me, Takes that dark damsel on his knee.

dig my grave both wide and deep, wide and deep, Put tomb-stones at my head and feet, head and feet, And on my breast carve a tur-tle dove, To sig-ni-fy I died of love.

Fare thee well, for I must leave thee, Do not

69

{|m .d' :d' .d' |d' .s :m m |f .t :t .t |t .s :l .t}

let the part-ing grieve thee, And re-mem-ber that the best of friends must

{|d' :l |s :—.s s :—.s |l .s :fe .s |m .s :s .s |s :—.s}

part, must part. A-dieu, a-dieu, kind friends, a-dieu, a-dieu, a-dieu, I

{|s :—.s |l .s :fe .s |r :s .,s |s .f :m .r |d :m |s :d' .d'}

cresc.

can no long-er stay with you, stay with you; I'll hang my harp on a

cresc.

D %

{|r .d' :t .d' |l :—.d' t :—.t |t .s :l .t |d' :— |— : .m ||}

weep-ing wil-low tree, And may the world go well with thee.___ 2. He
3. Oh

Fine. D %

The Little Brown Jug

By R. A. EASTBURN

Moderato   Doh is C.

1. My wife and I liv'd all a-lone, In a lit-tle log hut we call'd our own; She lov'd gin, and I lov'd rum,—I tell you what, we'd lots of fun. Ha, ha, ha, you and me, Lit-tle brown jug, don't I love thee; Ha, ha, ha, you and me, Lit-tle brown jug, don't I love thee.

2. 'Tis you who make my friends my foes, 'Tis you who make me wear old clothes; Here you are, so near my nose, So tip her up and down she goes.—*Chorus.*

3. When I go toiling to my farm,
I take little "Brown Jug" under my arm;
I place it under a shady tree,
Little "Brown Jug" 'tis you and me.—*Chorus.*

4. If all the folks in Adam's race,
Were gathered together in one place;
Then I'd prepare to shed a tear,
Before I'd part from you, my dear.—*Chorus.*

5. If I'd a cow that gave such milk,
I'd clothe her in the finest silk;
I'd feed her on the choicest hay,
And milk her forty times a day.—*Chorus.*

6. The rose is red, my nose is, too,
The violet's blue, and so are you;
And yet I guess before I stop,
We'd better take another drop.—*Chorus.*

This arrangement Copyright 1927 by Keith Prowse & Co., Ltd.

The animals went in two by two

American Tune

In march time

1. The an-i-mals went in two by two, Hur-rah! Hur-rah! The el-e-phant and the kang-a-roo, Hur-rah! Hur-rah! The an-i-mals went in two by two, The el-e-phant and the Kang-a-roo, And they all went in-to the Ark For to get out of the rain. And they all went in-to the ark For to get out of the rain.

2. The an-i-mals went in three by three, Hur-rah! Hur-rah! The wasp the ant and the bumble bee, Hur-rah! Hur-rah! The an-i-mals went in three by three, The wasp and the ant and the bum-ble bee, And they all went in-to the Ark

3.
The animals went in four by four,
The great hippopotamus stuck in the door.

4.
The animals went in five by five,
By eating each other they kept alive.

5.
The animals went in six by six,
They turned out the monkey because of his tricks.

6.
The animals went in seven by seven,
The little pig thought he was going to heaven.

This arrangement Copyright 1927 by Keith Prowse & Co., Ltd.

Camptown Races

S. C. FOSTER

Moderato — Key D

1. De Camp-town la - dies sing dis song, Doo - dah! Doo - dah! De Camp-town race-track five miles long, Doo - dah, doo - dah day! I came down dah wid my hat caved in, Doo - dah! long-tail fil-ly and de big black hoss, Doo - dah! Doo - dah! Dey fly de track and dey both cut a - cross, Doo - dah, doo - dah day! De blind hoss stickin' in a big mud hole, Doo - dah!

Doo - dah! I go back home wid a pock-et full of tin,
Doo - dah! Can't touch de bot-tom wid a ten - foot pole,

Doo - dah, doo - dah - day！
Doo - dah, doo - dah - day！

CHORUS

Gwine to run all night! Gwine to run all day! I'll bet my money on de bob-tail nag, Some-bod-y bet on de bay. 2. De

Old muley cow came on de track — Doodah, *etc.*
De bob-tail fling her ober his back,— Doodah-day!
Den fly along like a railroad car— Doodah, *etc.*
Runnin' a race wid a shootin' star — Doodah-day!
  Gwine to run all night! *etc.*

See dem flyin' on a ten-mile heat — Doodah, *etc.*
Round de race-track, den repeat — Doodah-day!
I win my money on de bob-tail nag — Doodah, *etc.*
I keep my money in an old tow bag — Doodah-day!
  Gwine to run all night! *etc.*

Marching through Georgia

In March time

By HENRY C. WORK

Key B♭

1. Bring the good old bu-gle, boys, we'll sing an-oth-er song,
2. How the dark-ies shout-ed when they heard the joy-ful sound;
3. Yes, and there were Un-ion men who wept with joy-ful tears,

Sing it with a spir-it that will start the world a-long,
How the turk-eys gob-bled which our com-mis-sa-ry found;
When they saw the hon-oured flag they had not seen for years;

Sing it as we used to sing it, fif-ty thou-sand strong,
How the sweet po-ta-toes e-ven started from the ground,
Hard-ly could they be re-strained from breaking forth in cheers,

4. "Sherman's dashing Yankee boys will never reach the coast,"
   So the saucy rebels said, and 'twas no idle boast;
   Had they not forgot, alas, to reckon with the host,
   While we were marching through Georgia.
         Hurrah! hurrah! *etc.*

5. So we made a thoroughfare for Freedom and her train,
   Sixty miles in latitude, three hundred to the main;
   Treason fled before us, for resistance was in vain,
   While we were marching through Georgia.
         Hurrah! hurrah! *etc.*

My Old Kentucky Home

S. C. FOSTER

Moderato — Key F

1. The sun shines bright in the old Kentuck-y home, 'Tis summer, the dark-ies are gay; The corn-top's ripe and the mea-dow's in the bloom, While the birds make mus-ic all the day; The

   hunt no more for the 'pos-sum and the coon, On the mea-dow, the hill and the shore; They sing no more by the glim-mer of the moon, On the bench by the old cab-in door; The

77

{ |m :m |d :r .,m |f .,m:f ,l.-|s : .f |m .r : .d |d .t, : .d |r :—|— : .r }

young folks roll on the lit-tle cab-in floor, All merry, all happy and bright; By'n
day goes by like a sha-dow o'er the heart, With sorrow where all was de-light; The

{ |m :m |d :r .,m |f .,m:f ,l |s :d .r |m .,d:f .m |r :—.d |d :—|— : }

bye hard times come a-knocking at the door, } Then my old Ken-tuck-y home, Good-night.—
time has come when the dark-ies have to part, }

CHORUS

{ |s :—.m |f :—.l |s .m:— |r |d :—.r |d :—.l, |d :—|— :.d .r }
                                                                                                                                    cresc.

Weep no more, my la-dy, O weep no more to-day! We will

D. %

{ |m :m |d :r .,m |f .,m:f .l |s :d .,r |m .,d:f .m |r :r .,d |d :—|— :.m || }
                                                                                                     rit.

sing one song for the old Ken-tuck-y home, For the old Kentucky home far a-way.— 2. They

D. %

John Brown's Body

March Song of the American War

Moderato — Doh is C

1. John Brown's bo-dy lies a-mould'ring in the grave, John Brown's bo-dy lies a-mould'ring in the grave, John Brown's bo-dy lies a-mould'ring in the grave, His soul is march-ing on.

    The stars of heav-en are look-ing kind-ly down, The stars of heav-en are look-ing kind-ly down, The stars of heav-en are look-ing kind-ly down, On the grave of old John Brown.

CHORUS

Glo-ry! glo-ry! Hal-le-lu-jah! Glo-ry! glo-ry! Hal-le-lu-jah! Glo-ry! glo-ry! Hal-le-lu-jah! His soul is march-ing on!

3. He's gone to be a soldier in the army of the Lord,
   His soul is marching on.
4. John Brown's knapsack is strapp'd upon his back,
   His soul is marching on.
5. His pet lambs will meet him on the way,
   And they'll go marching on.
6. We'll hang Jeff Davis on a sour apple tree,
   As we go marching on.

This arrangement Copyright 1927 by Keith Prowse & Co., Ltd.

My Bonnie

American Song

Moderato — Key B♭

1. My Bonnie is over the ocean,
   My Bonnie is over the sea,
   My Bonnie is over the ocean,
   O bring back my Bonnie to me.

   Bring back, bring back,
   Bring back my Bonnie to me, to me,
   Bring back, bring back,
   O bring back my Bonnie to me!

2. O blow ye winds over the ocean,
   O blow ye winds over the sea,
   O blow ye winds over the ocean,
   And bring back my Bonnie to me.
   Bring back, etc.

3. Last night as I lay on my pillow,
   Last night as I lay on my bed,
   Last night as I lay on my pillow,
   I dreamed that my Bonnie was dead.
   Bring back, etc.

4. The winds have blown over the ocean,
   The winds have blown over the sea,
   The winds have blown over the ocean,
   And brought back my Bonnie to me.
   Bring back, etc.

Polly-Wolly-Doodle

Allegretto.

1. Oh, I went down South for to see my Sal; Sing "Pol-ly-Wol-ly-Doo-dle" all the day! My Sal-ly am a live-ly gal, Sing "Pol-ly-Wol-ly-Doo-dle" all the day! Fare thee

Sal she am a maid-en fair; Sing "Pol-ly-Wol-ly-Doo-dle" all the day! With laugh-ing eyes and cur-ly hair, Sing "Pol-ly-Wol-ly-Doo-dle" all the day! Fare thee

3
Oh! I came to a river, an' I couldn't get across,
  Sing "Polly-wolly-doodle," all the day.
An' I jumped upon a nigger, for I thought he was a hoss,
  Sing "Polly-wolly-doodle," all the day. *(Chorus)*

4
Oh! a grasshopper sittin' on a railroad track,
  Sing "Polly-wolly-doodle," all the day.
A pickin' his teef wid a carpet tack,
  Sing "Polly-wolly-doodle," all the day. *(Chorus)*

5
Behind de barn, down on my knees,
  Sing "Polly-wolly-doodle," all the day.
I thought I heard a chicken sneeze,
  Sing "Polly-wolly-doodle," all the day. *(Chorus)*

6
He sneezed so hard wid de hoopin'-cough,
  Sing "Polly-wolly-doodle," all the day.
He sneezed his head an' his tail right off,
  Sing "Polly-wolly-doodle," all the day. *(Chorus)*

The old folks at home

Words & Music by STEPHEN C. FOSTER

Key D

Andante

{ :m :- |r :d :m .r }

1. Way down up - on the
2. All round the lit - tle
3. One lit - tle hut a -

{ |d :d' |l .d' :- |s :- |m :- .d |r :- |- : |m :- |r .d :m .r |d :d' |l .d' :- }

Swan-ee riv-er, Far, far a - way,___ There's where my heart is turn-ing ev - er,
farm I wan-der'd When I was young,___ Then ma - ny hap-py days I squander'd
mong the bush-es, One that I love___ Still sad-ly to my mem'ry rush-es,

{ |s :m .,d |r :r |d :- |- : |m :- |r .d :m .r |d :d' |l .d' :- |s :- |m :d |r :- |- : }

There's where the old folks stay.___ All up and down the whole cre-a-tion, Sad - ly I roam,___
Man - ny the songs I sung.___ When I was playing with my brother, Hap - py was I,___
No mat-ter where I rove.___ When shall I see the bees a - humming, All round the comb,___

{ |m :- |r .d :m .r |d :d' |l .d' :- |s :m .,d |r :m .,r |d :- |- : |t :- |d' |r' :s |s :- .l |s :d' }
cresc.

Still longing for the old plan-ta-tion, And for the old folks at home.___ All the world is sad and dreary,
Oh! take me to my kind old mother There let me live and die.___
When shall I hear the ban-jo thrumming Down in my good old home.___

{ |d' :l |f :l |s :- |- : |m :- |r .d |m .r |d :d' |l .d' |s :m .,d |r :m .,r |d :- |- : }
dim.

Ev-'ry where I roam,___ Oh, dark-ies how my heart grows weary, Far from the old folks at home.___

D.%

This arrangement Copyright 1927 by Keith Prowse & Co., Ltd

Poor Old Joe

Words & Music by STEPHEN C. FOSTER

Andante Doh is D.

1. Gone are the days when my heart was young and gay;
2. Why do I weep, when my heart should feel no pain?
3. Where are the hearts once so hap-py and so free? The

Gone are my friends from the cot-ton fields a-way;
Why do I sigh that my friends come not a-gain?
child-ren so dear, that I held up-on my knee?

Gone from the earth to a bet-ter land I know,
Griev-ing for forms now de-part-ed long a-go,
Gone to the shore where my soul has long'd to go,

I hear their gen-tle voic-es call-ing "Poor old Joe!"

CHORUS (Chorus in four parts)

I'm coming, I'm coming, for my head is bend-ing low, I hear their gentle voic-es call-ing "Poor old Joe!"

Fine

This arrangement Copyright 1927 by Keith Prowse & Co., Ltd.

Swing low, sweet chariot

Moderato

Swing low, sweet char-i-ot, Com-ing for to car-ry me home. Swing low, sweet char-i-ot, Com-ing for to car-ry me home.

This arrangement Copyright 1927 by Keith Prowse & Co., Ltd.

3. The brightest day that ever I saw,
   Coming for to carry me home,
   When Jesus washed my sins away,
   Coming for to carry me home.
   Swing low, *etc.*

4. I'm sometimes up and sometimes down,
   Coming for to carry me home,
   But still my soul feels heavenly bound,
   Coming for to carry me home.
   Swing low, *etc.*

So early in de morning

Moderato Key E♭

1. South Carolina's a sultry clime, Where we used to work in the summer-time, Massa 'neath the shade would lay, While we poor niggers toil'd all day.
2. When I was young I used to wait, On massa's table lay de plate, Pass de bottle when him dry, Brush away de blue tail'd fly.
3. Now massa's dead and gone to rest, Of all de massas he was best; I nebber seede like since I was born, Miss him now he's dead and gone.

CHORUS

So early in de morning, So early in de morning, So early in de morning, Before de break of day. So early in de morning, So early in de morning, So early in de morning, Before de break of day.

Aloha Oe
(Farewell to Thee)
HAWAIIAN SONG

Composed by
H. M. QUEEN LILINOKALANI.
Key A

Moderato
Proudly

Ha-a-heo ka u-a i na pa-li Ke nihi a-e-la ka-na-he-le E ha-
swept the rain-cloud by the cliff As on it gli-ded thro' the trees Still

li-a-nu-ka li-ko Pu-a a-hi-hi le hu-a-o u-ka. A-
fol-low-ing with grief the li-ko, The a-hi-hi le hua of the vale. Fare-

CHORUS

-lo-ha oe a-lo-ha oe E ke o-na-o-na no-ho i-ka li-po A'
-well to thee, fare-well to thee, Thou charming one who dwells a-mong the bow-ers, One

fond em-brace a ho-i a-e au Un-til we meet a-gain.
fond em-brace be-fore I now de-part, Un-til we meet a-gain.

Alouette
(The Lark)

French-Canadian Song

Moderato

Alouette, gentille Alouette, Alouette, Je te plumerai. Je te plumerai le bec, Je te plumerai le bec. Ah! le bec, Ah! le bec.

plumerai les pattes, Je te plumerai les pattes. Ah! les pattes, Ah! les pattes. Ah!

Alouette, gentille Alouette, Alouette, Je te plumerai. 2. Je te

3. Je te plumerai le dos, *(sing twice)*
   Ah! le dos. *etc.*

4. Je te plumerai la tête, (,,)
   Ah! la tête. *etc.*

5. Je te plumerai la "falle", *(sing twice)*
   Ah! la "falle." *etc.*

6. Je te plumerai la queue, (,,)
   Ah! la queue. *etc.*

Note: bec *(beak)*. pattes *(legs)*. dos *(back)*. tête *(head)*. falle *(breast)*. queue *(tail)*

This arrangement Copyright 1927 by Keith Prowse & Co., Ltd.

A Canadian Boat Song

Words and Music by THOMAS MOORE

1. Faint-ly as tolls the eve-ning chime, Our voic-es keep tune, and our oars keep time, Our voic-es keep tune, and our oars keep time; Soon as the woods on shore look dim, We'll sing at Saint Ann's our part-ing hymn. Row, broth-ers, row! the stream runs fast, The Rapids are near, and the day-light's past, The Rapids are near, and the day-light's past.

2. Why should we yet our sail un-furl? There is not a breath the blue wave to curl, There is not a breath the blue wave to curl. But when the wind blows off the shore, Oh! sweet-ly we'll rest our wea-ry oar. Blow, bree-zes, blow! the stream runs fast, The Rapids are near, and the day-light's past, The Rapids are near, and the day-light's past.

This arrangement Copyright 1927 by Keith Prowse & Co., Ltd.

Clementine

Moderato — Key G

1. In a cavern, in a cañon, Excavating for a mine,
Dwelt a miner, forty-niner, And his daughter Clementine.

CHORUS
O my darling! O my darling! O my darling Clementine!
Thou art lost and gone for ever, Dreadful sorry, Clementine!

2. Light she was and like a fairy,
And her shoes were number nine;
Herring boxes without topses,
Sandals were for Clementine.

3. Drove she ducklings to the water,
Ev'ry morning just at nine;
Hit her foot against a splinter,
Fell into the foaming Brine.

4. Saw her lips above the water
Blowing bubbles mighty fine;
But alas! I was no swimmer,
So I lost my Clementine. *(Chorus)*

5. In a Churchyard near the cañon,
Where the myrtle doth entwine,
There grow roses and other posies
Fertilized by Clementine. *(Chorus)*

6. Then the miner, forty-niner,
Soon began to peak and pine;
Thought he "oughter jine" his daughter—
Now he's with his Clementine. *(Chorus)*

7. In my dreams she still doth haunt me,
Robed in garments soaked in brine;
Though in life, I used to hug her,
Now she's dead, I'll draw the line. *(Chorus)*

Cock Robin

Andante Key G

1. Who kill'd Cock Robin? I said the Sparrow, With my bow and ar-row, I kill'd Cock Robin.
2. Who saw him die? I said the fly, With my lit-tle eye, I saw him die.
3. Who'll toll the bell? I said the Bull, Be-cause I can pull, I'll toll the bell.

CHORUS

All the birds of the air fell a-sigh-ing and a-sobbing, When they heard of the death of poor Cock Ro-bin, When they heard of the death of poor Cock Ro-bin.

4.
Who'll dig his grave?
I, said the Owl,
With my little trowel,
I'll dig his grave.—*Cho.*

5.
Who'll be the parson?
I, said the Rook;
With my little book,
I'll be the parson.—*Cho.*

6.
Who'll be chief mourner?
I, said the Dove,
I mourn for my love,
I'll be chief mourner.—*Cho.*

This arrangement Copyright 1927 by Keith Prowse & Co., Ltd.

Good Night, ladies!

The Keel Row

Allegretto Key E♭

1. As I cam' doon the Sand-gate, the Sand-gate, the Sand-gate, As I cam' doon the Sand-gate I heard a las-sie sing:— O mer-ry may the keel row, the keel row, the keel row, O mer-ry may the keel row, The ship my lad-die's in.

2. He wears a blue bon-net a bon-net, a bon-net, He wears a blue bon-net, A dim-ple in his chin.

3. He's com-ing soon to meet me, to meet me, to meet me, He's com-ing soon to meet me From yon ship in the Tyne.

The Maple leaf for ever.
(The National Song of Canada)

Words and Music by ALEXANDER MUIR

Con spirito.

Key A♭

1. In days of yore from Britain's shore
Wolfe the dauntless hero came, And planted firm Britannia's flag On Canada's fair domain! Here

Merry England's far-famed land
May kind Heaven sweetly smile; God bless Old Scotland evermore, And Ireland's Emerald Isle! Then

95

may it wave, our boast, our pride, And joined in love to-gether, The
swell the song, both loud and long, Till rocks and for-est quiv-er, God

CHORUS

This-tle, Shamrock, Rose en-twine The Ma-ple leaf for ev-er! The
save our King, and Heav-en bless The Ma-ple leaf for ev-er!

Ma-ple leaf, our Em-blem dear, The Ma-ple leaf for ev-er! God

save our King, and Heav-en bless The Ma-ple leaf for ev-er! 2. On

Sweet Genevieve

GEORGE COOPER. HENRY TUCKER.

1. O Genevieve! I'd give the world To live again the lovely past! The rose of youth was dew impearl'd But now it withers in the blast. I see thy face in ev'ry dream, My

Genevieve! My early love, The years but make thee dearer far! My heart shall never, never rove; Thou art my only guiding star. For me the past has no regret, What-

97

waking thoughts are full of thee; Thy glance is in the
-e'er the years may bring to me; I bless the hour when
starry beam That falls along the summer sea.
first we met, The hour that gave me love and thee.

CHORUS

O Gen-e-vieve, sweet Gen-e-vieve! The days may come, the days may go, But still the hands of mem'ry weave The bliss-ful dreams of long a-go. 2. Fair

Some Folks do

S. C. FOSTER

Moderato

1. Some folks like to sigh, Some folks do, some folks do; Some folks long to die, But that's not me nor you. Long live the mer-ry, merry heart That laughs by night and day, Like the Queen of mirth, No mat-ter what some folks say.

2. Some folks fear to smile, Some folks do, some folks do; Oth-ers laugh thro' guile, But that's not me nor you. Long live etc.

3. Some folks fret and scold, Some folks do, some folks do; They'll soon be dead and cold, But that's not me nor you. Long live etc.

4.
Some folks get grey hairs,
  Some folks do, some folks do;
Brooding o'er their cares,
  But that's not me nor you.
    Long live *etc.*

5.
Some folks toil and save
  Some folks do, some folks do;
To buy themselves a grave,
  But that's not me nor you.
    Long live *etc.*

Where are you going, My pretty maid?

99

Moderato   Key G

1. Where are you go-ing, my pret-ty maid?
2. Shall I come with you, my pret-ty maid?

Where are you go-ing, my pret-ty maid? "I'm going a milk-ing, Sir," she said,
Shall I come with you, my pret-ty maid? "Oh, yes, if you please, kind Sir," she said,

"Sir," she said, "Sir," she said, "I'm go-ing a milk-ing, Sir," she said.
"Sir," she said, "Sir," she said, "Oh, yes, if you please, kind Sir," she said.

3
What is your father, my pretty maid?
What is your father, my pretty maid?
"My father's a farmer, Sir," she said,
"Sir," she said, "Sir," she said,
"My father's a farmer, Sir," she said.

4
Shall I marry you, my pretty maid?
Shall I marry you, my pretty maid?
"Oh, yes, if you please, kind Sir," she said,
"Sir," she said, "Sir," she said,
"Oh, yes, if you please, kind Sir" she said.

5
And what is your fortune, my pretty maid?
And what is your fortune, my pretty maid?
"My face is my fortune, Sir," she said,
"Sir," she said, "Sir," she said,
"My face is my fortune, Sir," she said,

6
Then I can't marry you, my pretty maid,
Then I can't marry you, my pretty maid.
"Nobody ax'd you, "Sir," she said,
"Sir," she said, "Sir," she said,
"Nobody ax'd you, "Sir," she said.

This arrangement Copyright 1927 by Keith Prowse & Co., Ltd.

Hark, the bonny Christ Church Bells.

Dr ALDRICH

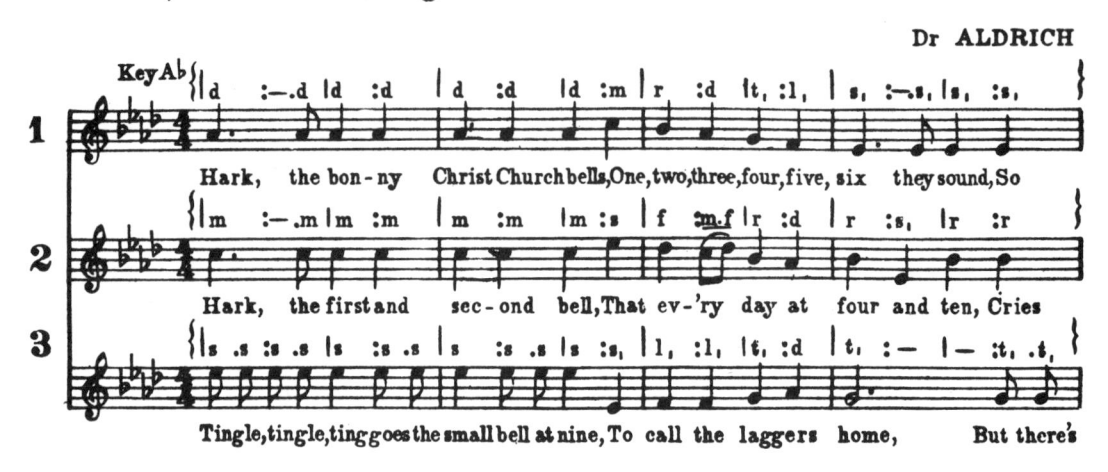

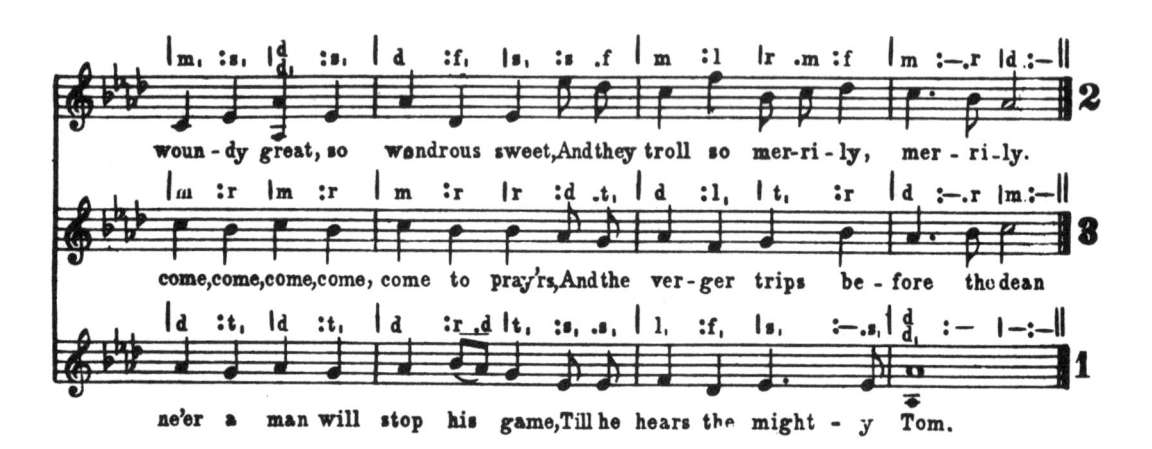

Hark, the bonny Christ Church bells, One, two, three, four, five, six they sound, So woundy great, so wondrous sweet, And they troll so merrily, merrily.

Hark, the first and second bell, That ev'ry day at four and ten, Cries come, come, come, come, come to pray'rs, And the verger trips before the dean

Tingle, tingle, ting goes the small bell at nine, To call the laggers home, But there's ne'er a man will stop his game, Till he hears the mighty Tom.

Haste thee, Nymph

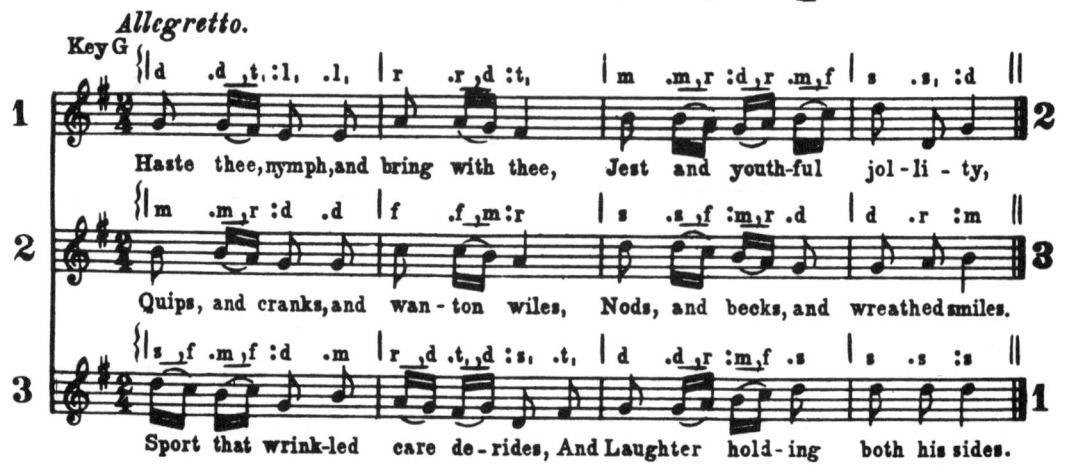

Allegretto.

Haste thee, nymph, and bring with thee, Jest and youthful jollity,

Quips, and cranks, and wanton wiles, Nods, and becks, and wreathed smiles.

Sport that wrinkled care derides, And Laughter holding both his sides.

Dame! get up and bake your pies

Moderato

1. Dame! get up and bake your pies, Bake your pies, Bake your pies;
2. Dame! what makes your maidens lie, Maidens lie, maidens lie;

Dame! get up and bake your pies } On Christmas day in the morning?
Dame! what makes your maidens lie }

3. Dame! what makes your ducks to die,
   Ducks to die, ducks to die;
   Dame! what makes your ducks to die,
   On Christmas-day in the morning?

4. Their wings are cut and they cannot fly,
   Cannot fly, cannot fly;
   Their wings are cut and they cannot fly,
   On Christmas-day in the morning.

Hickory, Dickory, Dock!

Moderato.

Hickory, Dickory, Dock! The mouse ran up the clock; The clock struck one, The mouse was gone, Hickory, Dickory, Dock!

Jack and Jill

Moderato.
Key D

Jack and Jill went up the hill, To fetch a pail of water;
Jack fell down and broke his crown, And Jill came tumb-ling aft-er.

Little Bo-Peep

Moderato
Key F

Lit-tle Bo-Peep has lost her sheep, And can-not tell where to find them;
Leave them a-lone, And they'll come home, And bring their tails be-hind them.

Rock-a-bye Baby

103

Slowly

Rock-a-bye Ba-by, on the tree top, When the wind blows the cra-dle will rock;

When the bough breaks the cra-dle will fall, Down will come cra-dle, ba-by and all.

K P. 3176

When good King Arthur ruled this land

Moderato

1. When good King Ar-thur ruled this land, He was a good-ly King; He stole three pecks of bar-ley meal, To make a bag pud-ding. 2. A
bag pud-ding the Queen did make, And stuffed it full of plums; And in it put great lumps of fat, As big as my two thumbs. 3. The
King and Queen sat down to dine, And no-ble-men be-side; And what they could not eat that night, The Queen next morn-ing fried.

Abide with me

H. F. LYTE
W. H. MONK

1. Abide with me! fast falls the eventide;
   The darkness deepens, Lord, with me abide!
   When other helpers fail, and comforts flee,
   Help of the helpless, O abide with me!

2. I need Thy presence ev'ry passing hour;
   What but Thy grace can foil the tempter's pow'r?
   Who like Thyself my guide and stay can be?
   Thro' cloud and sunshine, O abide with me!

3. I fear no foe, with Thee at hand to bless;
   Ills have no weight, and tears no bitterness;
   Where is death's sting? Where, grave, thy victory?
   I triumph still, if Thou abide with me!

This arrangement Copyright 1927 by Keith Prowse & Co., Ltd.

Glorious things of thee are spoken

HAYDN

1. *f* Glorious things of thee are spoken, Zion, city of our God;
2. *mf* See, the streams of living waters, Springing from eternal love,
3. Round each habitation hov'ring, See the cloud and fire appear,
4. *p* Saviour, since of Zion's city I, through grace, a member am,

He Whose word cannot be broken Form'd thee for His own abode.
Well supply thy sons and daughters, And all fear of want remove.
For a glory and a cov'ring—Showing that the Lord is near.
Let the world deride or pity, I will glory in Thy Name.

On the Rock of ages founded, What can shake thy sure repose?
Who can faint while such a river Ever flows their thirst to assuage;
Thus they march, the pillar leading, Light by night and shade by day;
Fading is the world's best pleasure, All its boasted pomp and show;

With salvation's walls surrounded, Thou mayst smile at all thy foes.
Grace, which like the Lord the Giver, Never fails from age to age?
Daily on the manna feeding Which He gives them when they pray.
f Solid joys and lasting treasure None but Zion's children know. A-men

Grace
(FOR THESE AND ALL THY MERCIES)

From the "LAUDI SPIRITUALI"

For these and all Thy mercies given, We bless and praise Thy name, O Lord. May we receive them with thanksgiving, Ever trusting in Thy Word: To Thee alone be honour, glory, Now and henceforth for evermore. Amen.

*Lo! heaven and earth

JOACHIM NEANDER (1679)
(Translated by Catherine Winkworth)

D. KORNER (1628)
(Arr. by Ernest Newton)

Paternoster

1. Lo, heaven and earth, and sea and air, Alleluia! Their maker's glory all declare; Alleluia! And thou my soul awake and sing, Alleluia! To Him thy praises also bring.
2. Through Him the glorious source of day Alleluia! Drives all the clouds of night away; Alleluia! The pomp of stars, the moon's soft light, Alleluia! Praise Him through all the silent night. Alleluia! Alleluia! Alleluia! Alleluia!
3. O Lord, how wondrously dost Thou Alleluia! Unfold Thyself to us e'en now! Alleluia! Oh, grave it deeply on my heart Alleluia! What I am, Lord, and what Thou art!

By kind permission of Messrs Pitman Hart & Co.

Nearer my God to Thee

SARAH ADAMS J. B. DYKES

1. Near-er, my God, to Thee, Near-er to Thee, E'en though it be a cross, That rais-eth me; Still all my song shall be,
2. Though like the wan-der-er, The sun gone down, Dark-ness comes o-ver me, My rest a stone; Yet in my dreams I'd be
3. There let my way ap-pear Steps un-to heaven, All that Thou send-est me In mer-cy given, Angels to beck-on me,
4. Then, with my wa-king thoughts Bright with Thy praise, Out of my sto-ny griefs, Bethel I'll raise; So by my woes to be

Nearer, my God, to Thee, Nearer to Thee!

Old Hundredth

Rev. W. KETHE *Genevan Psalter*

1. All peo-ple that on earth do dwell, Sing to the Lord with cheer-ful voice; Him serve with fear, His praise forth tell, Come ye be-fore Him, and re-joice.
2. The Lord, ye know is God in-deed, With-out our aid He did us make; We are His flock, He doth us feed, And for His sheep He doth us take.
3. O en-ter then His gates with praise, Ap-proach with joy His courts un-to; Praise, laud, and bless His name al-ways, For it is seem-ly so to do.
4. For why? the Lord our God is good; His mer-cy is for ev-er sure; His truth at all times firm-ly stood, And shall from age to age en-dure.

These arrangements Copyright 1927 by Keith Prowse & Co Ltd

O Come, all ye faithful

1. O come, all ye faithful, Joyful and triumphant, O come ye, O come ye to Bethlehem; Come and behold Him Born the King of Angels;
2. God of God, Light of Light, Lo! He abhors not the Virgin's womb; Very God, Begotten, not created:
3. Sing, choirs of Angels, Sing in exultation, Sing, all ye citizens of Heav'n above: "Glory to God In the highest;"
4. Yea, Lord, we greet Thee, Born this happy morning; Jesu, to Thee be glory given; Word of the Father, Now in flesh appearing;

O come, let us adore Him, O come let us adore Him, O come let us adore Him, Christ the Lord. Amen.

O God, our help in ages past

Tune – St. Anne

1. O God, our help in ages past, Our hope for years to come,
   Our shelter from the storm-y blast, And our e-ter-nal home.
2. Be-neath the shad-ow of Thy throne Thy saints have dwelt se-cure;
   Suf-fi-cient is Thine arm a-lone, And our de-fence is sure.
3. Be-fore the hills in or-der stood, Or earth re-ceived her frame,
   From ev-er-last-ing Thou art God To end-less years the same.
4. A thous-and a-ges in Thy sight Are like an eve-ning gone;
   Short as the watch that ends the night Be-fore the ris-ing sun.

5. Time, like an ever rolling stream,
   Bears all its sons away;
   They fly forgotten, as a dream
   Dies at the opening day.

6. O God our help in ages past,
   Our hope for years to come,
   Be Thou our guard while troubles last,
   And our eternal home!

Glory to Thee, my God

THOMAS KEN — TALLIS

1. Glor-y to Thee, my God, this night For all the bless-ings of the light;
   Keep me, O keep me, King of Kings, Be-neath Thy own Al-migh-ty wings.
2. For-give me, Lord, for Thy dear Son, The ill that I this day have done,
   That with the world, my-self and Thee, I, ere I sleep, at peace may be.
3. Teach me to live, that I may dread The grave as lit-tle as my bed;
   Teach me to die, that so I may, Rise glori-ous at the aw-ful day.
4. O may my soul on Thee re-pose And may sweet sleep mine eye-lids close,
   Sleep that shall me more vigor-ous make To serve my God when I a-wake. A-men

mf 5. When in the night I sleepless lie,
   My soul with heavenly thoughts supply;
   Let no ill dreams disturb my rest,
   No powers of darkness me molest.

f 6. Praise God from Whom all blessings flow,
   Praise Him all creatures here below,
   Praise Him above, Angelic host,
   Praise FATHER, SON and HOLY GHOST.

These arrangements Copyright 1927 by Keith Prowse & Co., Ltd.

Praise, my Soul, the King of Heaven.

REGENT SQUARE
HENRY SMART.

1. Praise, my Soul, the King of Heaven, To His feet thy tribute bring; Ransomed, healed, restored, forgiven, Evermore His praises sing; Alleluia! Alleluia! Praise the everlasting King!

2. Praise Him for His grace and favour To our fathers in distress; Praise Him still the same as ever, Slow to chide and swift to bless: Alleluia! Alleluia! Glorious in His faithfulness.

3. Father-like, He tends and spares us, Well our feeble frame He knows; In His hands He gently bears us, Rescues us from all our foes: Alleluia! Alleluia! Widely yet His mercy flows.

4. Angels in the height, adore Him; Ye behold Him face to face; Saints triumphant, bow before Him, Gather'd in from ev'ry race: Alleluia! Alleluia! Praise with us the God of grace.

Vesper Hymn

THOMAS MOORE. *Russian Air*

1. Hark the Ves-per hymn is steal-ing O'er the wa-ters soft and clear; Near-er yet and near-er peal-ing, Soft it breaks up-on the ear. Ju-bi-la-te! Ju-bi-la-te! Ju-bi-la-te! A-men.
2. Now like moon-light waves re-treat-ing, To the shore it dies a-long; Now like an-gry sur-ges meet-ing, Breaks the min-gled tide of song. Ju-bi-la-te! Ju-bi-la-te! Ju-bi-la-te! A-men.
3. Once a-gain sweet voi-ces ring-ing, Loud-er still the mu-sic swells; While on sum-mer breez-es wing-ing, Comes the chime of Ves-per bells. Ju-bi-la-te! Ju-bi-la-te! Ju-bi-la-te! A-men.